Mapping the Muse:
A Bicentennial Look at Indiana Poetry

Introduction

Mapping the Muse: A Bicentennial Look at Indiana Poetry is the culmination of a project originated by Brick Street Poetry, Inc. designed to celebrate Indiana's 200th year by presenting a glimpse of poetry in Indiana. The *Birthday Book* project is an endorsed Bicentennial Legacy Project recognized by the Indiana Bicentennial Celebration 2016.

Mapping the Muse consists of poetry representing a wide range of experience: from every-day poets to university professors; from high school students to senior poets in their 90s; and a collaborative poem by a 5th grade class in Perry County.

Brick Street Poetry solicited the participation of libraries in each Indiana County through a partnership with the Indiana State Library. Participating libraries selected up to 5 poems and forwarded them to Brick Street Poetry. Poems selected for each county were judged by members of the Brick Street Board of Directors. A total of 59 counties are represented by individual poets.

In addition to poets from individual counties, the book includes poems and biographies from each of the four current and former poets laureate: George Kalamaras, Karen Kovacik, Norbert Krapf, and Joyce Brinkman.

Brick Street Poetry also solicited collaborative poems from three active groups of poets throughout the state: Indiana State Federation of Poetry Clubs; Prairie Writers Guild in Renssellaer; and an ad hoc group of poets who collaborated on a poem about 8 major Indiana rivers. A collaborative poem is one in which several poets contribute their efforts into a single poem, typically one stanza by each poet. The book's cover also provides a glimpse of a very small portion of a very long collaborative poem by Project 411, the result of an invitation from our current Poet Laureate George Kalamaras to poets and non-poets to contribute to a 411 line free-flowing poem.

Brick Street Poetry wishes to give special thanks to the Indiana State Library, who helped us initate the participation of libraries in each Indiana County; Kaylie Picket, our intern who helped coordinate library submissions; Triangle Printing Company in Indianapolis for printing *Mapping the Muse*; and donations received from: Carlee Alson, Stephen Anspach, Susie Beiman, David Best, Jared Carter, Penny Dunning, Christine Duttlinger, Dennis Greene, Colin Hawkins, Jackie Huppert, Connie Kingman, Karen Kovacik, Dolores Kramer, Donna Monday, Thomas O'Dore, Roger Pfingston, John Sherman, Susan Stiles, Suzanne Sturgeon, Gary Thompson, Carl Van Dorn, Shari Wagner, and The Prairie Writers Guild.

Barry Harris, Editor

Brick Street Poetry, Inc.

Brick Street Poetry Inc. is a tax-exempt non-profit organization under IRS Code 501(c)(3). Brick Street Poetry Inc. publishes the *Tipton Poetry Journal*, hosts the monthly poetry series *Poetry on Brick Street* (in Zionsville) and sponsors other poetry-related events.

Copyright 2015 by Brick Street Poetry

Mapping the Muse:
A Bicentennial Look at Indiana Poetry

Cover Illustration: Project 411

Appearing inside the Indiana map on this book's front cover, you can glimpse a very small portion of a very long poem which is the result of Project 411. Project 411 was initiated by Indiana's current poet laureate, George Kalamaras. George invited the Indiana public to contribute a line of poetry to Project 411, which collaboratively built a poem representing the 411 miles of the Wabash River.

Project 411 Participants:

D.L. Aghabekian, Stevens Amidon, Aleisha R. Balestri, Eric Baus, Nancy Botkin, Brad A. Bott, Tony Brewer, Joyce Brinkman, Michael Brockley, Marsha Browne, Caitlyn Bushnell, Madison Bushnell, Tasha N. Bushnell, Mary Ann Cain, Colleen Card, Dan Carpenter, Kay Castaneda, Curtis L. Crisler, Rick Cummings, Dawn Cunningham, Ellen Cutter, Julie Demoff-Larson, Donna S. Eckelbarger, Shannon Elward, Heather Fox, Rebecca Franklin, Sarah Fronczek, Helen Frost, Jeff Gundy, Janine Harrison, Amy Holston Hesting, Laurie Higi, Jenni Hout, Jackie Huppenthal, George Kalamaras, JL Kato, Charles Kelley, Megan King, Pat Kopanda, Karen Kovacik, Elizabeth Krajeck, Mary Kramer, Becca Lamarre, Marsi Lawson, Nancy Chen Long, Doris Lynch, Louise Magoon, Bryn Marlow, Michael Martone, Bonnie Maurer, Kathy Mayer, Aaron Michael McClaskey, Tracy Mishkin, Roger Mitchell, Aly Noble, Sandie Patterson, Deborah Petersen, Roger Pfingston, Richard Pflum, Janine Pickett, Nancy Pulley, Mary Quigley, Hugh Rettinger, Ron Riha, Stephen R. Roberts, Lucia Walton Robinson, Barbara Shoup, Nancy Simmonds, Kevin Stein, Christopher Stolle, Anthony Thieme, Amy Jo Trier-Walker, Katerina Tsiopos, Shari Wagner, Laurie Walls, Melanie Shifflett Ridner Warner, Kathryn Ann Young, Jordan Zandi

Participants in Project 411 are from these counties: Allen, Bartholomew, Brown, Delaware, Hamilton, Jackson, Jasper, Kosciusko, Lake, Madison, Marion, Marshall, Monroe, Noble, Porter, Ripley, St. Joseph, Tippecanoe, Wayne, Wells, and Whitley.

Also, participants formerly from Indiana now living elsewhere came from Bluffton, Ohio; Denver, Colorado; Jay, New York; Peoria, Illinois; San Jose, California; Tuscaloosa, Alabama; and Wilmington, North Carolina.

The entire text of the poem can be viewed at:

http://www.wabashwatershed.com/2015/11/01/project-411-unveiled/

Contents

Indiana's Poets Laureate 1

George Kalamaras (Current Indiana Poet Laureate 2014-) 2

Karen Kovacik (Indiana Poet Laureate 2012-2014) 4

Norbert Krapf (Indiana Poet Laureate 2008-2010) 6

Joyce Brinkman (Indiana Poet Laureate 2002-2008) 11

Following the Rivers' Flow: A Collaborative Poem by Joyce Brinkman, Mark Neely, Orlando Menes, Shari Wagner, Don Platt, Kevin McKelvey, Mitchell Douglas, Matthew Brennan, Marcus Wicker, Laurel Smith) 17

Prairie: A Collaborative Poem by The Prairie Writers Guild (John D. Groppe, Pat Kopanda, Carlee Tressel Alson, Marcia Smith-Wood, Maia Hawthorne, Shannon Anderson, Doris Myers, J. Patrick Lewis, Gus Nybergm Sally Nalbor, Alyssa Cook, Connie Kingman, Joyce Brinkman) 19

Indiana State Parks: A Collaborative Poem by Indiana Federation of Poetry Clubs (Joyce Brinkman, Alice Couch, Nancy Simmonds, S. Evan Walters, Marlene Million, Alys Caviness-Gober, Jenny Kalahar, Kathy Maves, Mary Couch) 25

Robert Ummel (Allen County) 29

Nancy Pulley (Bartholomew County) 30

Maddie Weimer (Benton County) 31

Brenda Miller (Boone County) 32

Keith Bradway (Brown County) 33

Christian Knoeller (Carroll County) 34

Marissa Rose (Delaware County) 35

Linda E. Reschly Schrock (Elkhart County) 36

Doug Easley (Fayette County) 37

F.A. Vickery (Fountain County) 38

Claire Eckstein (Franklin County) 40

Marie Julian (Gibson County) 41

Dan Fuller (Grant County) 42

Carol Ogdon (Greene County) 44

Stephen R. Roberts (Hamilton County) 45

Stacy Post (Hendricks County) 46

Robert Stephen Dicken (Henry County) 47

Lisa Fipps (Howard County) 48

Rosella Corll (Huntington County) 50

Carlee Tressel Alson (Jasper County) 52

Mable Jean Caylor (Jay County) 53

Kay Stokes (Jefferson County) 54

Jennifer Rockhold (Jennings County) 57

Mya Holbrook (Johnson County) 59

Laurel Smith (Knox County) 61

Carol Massat (La Grange County) 62

Jackie Huppenthal (Lake County) 63

Dondeena Caldwell (Madison County) 64

Richard Pflum (Marion County) 65

Norma Wideman (Miami County) 66

Leah Helen May (Monroe County) 67

Gerburg Garmann (Montgomery County) 68

Kelly McNeil (Morgan County) 69

John Lyttle (Owen County) 71

Joan Lunsford (Parke County) 72

Joan Goble's 2010 Cannelton Elementary 5th Grade Class (Perry County) 73

Ryan Fredric Steinbeck (Porter County) 75

Jessica Thompson (Posey County) 76

Mary Lee Gutwein (Pulaski County) 77

Joseph Heithaus (Putnam County) 79

Cathy May (Ripley County) 80

Don A. Wright (Rush County) 81

Thomas Alan Orr (Shelby County) 82

Peggy Brooks (Spencer County) 83

Carol Rupley (St. Joseph County) 85

Carol Grubbs (Starke County) 86

Nick Boone (Sullivan County) 87

B.J. Green (Switzerland County)... 89

Thomas O'Dore (Tippecanoe County) 90

Ben Rose (Tipton County) 91

Ruth Frasur (Union County) 92

Rob Griffith (Vanderburgh County) 95

Gary Cowan (Vermillion County) 96

Mark Minster (Vigo County) 97

Nancy Bell (Wabash County)... 99

Marcy Meyer Johnson (Warren County) 100

Betty A. Stanley (Washington County) 101

Patricia D. Drischel (Wayne County).............................. 102

Doug Sundling (Wells County) 103

Amy McVay Abbott (Whitley County) 104

Indiana's Poets Laureate

The Indiana Arts Commission, Former State Treasurer Joyce Brinkman, and Senator Theresa Lubbers developed Senate Bill 433, which formalized the role of Poet Laureate for Indiana in 2002.

The IAC is charged with selecting the Poet Laureate, providing an annual stipend and per diem, and working with the State Department of Education in scheduling appearances.

The Indiana Poet Laureate official duties include:

- Making presentations at schools, libraries, and other educational facilities
- Promoting poetry and writing to schools and communities across the state
- Providing advice on how to promote poetry and writing to the IAC and other organizations

There have been four Indiana Poets Laureate: Joyce Brinkman, Norbert Krapf, Karen Kovacik and George Kalamaras. Each Poet Laureate was asked to contribute a poem for this Bicentennial Project. Their poems, and their biographies, follow.

Sparrow to Hound

George Kalamaras (Current Indiana Poet Laureate 2014-   )

Based on a photo of several dogs, a couple of which are hounds, staring through the wood planks of a fence in the snow—"Dog Kennels, Peru, Indiana," January 2, 1925

Sparrow should be a verb. I write poems
because I am a man. Almost
human. Almost dog. Sometimes
I wake up. I rarely wake
down. Most times, I shake snow
from my coat and wake unto the world.
Sparrow should be
an adverb. I write all actions
of the canary back into the throat. Sparrow
should be a weed, a cabbage, tea leaves
waiting to be read in the cup. I write my future
as if it were my last. One of the great unknown
inventions of Nikola Tesla
was water. Was an emery board
used to tune a violin. Was hound-song
beamed electrically from Peru,
Indiana, to the underground chambers
of the Gobi. I wish my brain could wake down.
Stay kenneled on one thought or other. Not drift
like hound snout leaf to leaf. Hound should be
a verb. Wait—perhaps it is, if—like captured
lightning—it's bound to a sentence like:
George is hounding George again. My name
like wood planks on either side,
enough to corral anything, keep
any sentence splinter-stuck in what was.
In what could have been. Sparrow should be
the world. The world according to Tesla,
where the longings of Indiana hounds awaken the moon
turning desert mites thousands of miles away.
I wish I was thousands of miles away, or even here,
completely, right now. To be so present in a place,
like Han Shan acquiring the name *Cold Mountain*

Mapping the Muse

from twenty-three years of meditating on and becoming
one with that mountain. Han Shan seeds
and does not seed Cold Mountain. Cold Mountain
breeds and does not breed Han Shan. Han Shan should be
a verb. An action word meaning, *to live*
with the intensity of a hound, cold-scented snout
to the ground. Here I go again, hypnotizing
water. Measuring the moist of my mouth
against the voltage of a sparrow slinging
through bamboo toward the sun.
Coaxing the canary back into the canals
of the throat. *My* throat. If I had four
throats, like the trebling of a cow's
cud moving from stomach three
to stomach four. If I had a hermit hut
and the warmth of Cold Mountain,
a meadow of waking down
rather than up. Of reading, say,
the tea leaves wise. When you pour
boiling water from the kettle
across the leaves, the steeping
as they release is called *the agony of the leaves.*
Odd, since what they give replenishes. Agony
should be a verb. One we throw out.
Collectively. Or at least dandle
during moments of what we gnaw on
as the woe of the world moves
one person to the next. Cow stomach
to cow stomach. Canary
to kennel. Sparrow to hound

(*for Tom Hastings*)

The Book Nook Piano: "Hoagy Liked Me Hot"

Karen Kovacik (Indiana Poet Laureate 2012-2014)

I didn't care who touched me
       long as they could play—
white hands, black hands
       pinging from treble to bass.
What did I know of crosses
       at the edge of town
lit by men in hoods who'd strip
       my keyboard of sharps?

Hoagy liked me hot. Heavy
       thumb after the chord
just like Reg DuValle showed.
       Reggie's Blackbyrds headlined
at Indy's hottest spots,
       and his and Oletha's house
served as hotel for the likes of Ellington
       frozen out by Jim Crow.

Back then, skinny Hoag lived the blues,
       ankle deep in slush
during shifts at the cement plant.
       He'd trolley to the DuValles on Harlan
to soak up Reggie's swing
       while Oletha offered pot roast, cobbler.
"Make that harmony holler,"
       Reg taught. "Till it sounds just *right*."

Hoag and I met at the Book Nook,
       hangout for poets and jazzhounds.
during his days at IU Law.
       They pelted us with grapefruit rinds
when Hoagy hunted for "Stardust."
       Said he didn't write melodies—
they showed up on my keys.
       In every weather he made me sing:

4

drizzly moods of last dollars,
      arpeggios smuggled in
with westside Granny's pints,
      Dada cyclones of movie tunes.
Hoagy'd practice jazz slides for dances
      down at Showers Furniture
where sanders and planers off the clock
      doodled and mooched, hands on hips,
no daylight 'tween them and their girls.

You could call it a second Civil War—
      Nordic types in sheets burning
a gash between the races
      while lovers of jazz and gin
crossed the color line
      a dozen times a day.
I watched this Doctor of Law
      hopscotch to black-and-tans,
ditch Columbia Club for Cotton.

Later my pedal stuck
      and my old spruce soundboard
came unglued. Reg DuValle
      caught the blues
working double shifts at Linco Gas
      and jazz, no time for sleep.
And Hoagy rode that color line
      ebony and ivory express
all the way to the top.

Indiana Shadows and Light

Norbert Krapf (Indiana Poet Laureate 2008-2010)

1. Southern Indiana

Into the woods I came to listen
so I could see. My father
heard but I saw better.
Droppings of hickory shells

said squirrels before a tail appeared.
Came to know names of shagbark hickory,
white oak, walnut, beech, pig hickory
as food trees. Stepped lightly toe first

so no dry leaf or branch said a thing.
Always looked up, ears wide open.
From him I learned beauty, shapes
of trunks and branches, configurations

of leaf clusters and flash of red tail
that said fox squirrel. Some trees
and woods older than others,
immersed in ancient shadow.

Entering time outside of time.
Feeling connected with oldest of ways.
Shade deepening into darkening dusk.
Bird tweet and whisper as late prayers

remaining from a time before I came
to be born. Before I could hear
and see. Before words came into
my mouth for tongue to taste.

2. On the Edge of the Prairie

Four hours by car to the north
on the edge of the prairie
I came into the life of books.
Sometimes rode the Monon
from the hills of the south
into land that looked and felt flat
though it did begin to undulate
and wind could howl and whip

like I had never heard or felt.
Heard the blab of wheels
on pavement and felt the splendid
silent sun on my slender shoulders

in the pages of Walt Whitman's
Leaves of Grass. Saw corn grow
in every direction. Baptized in green.
Consecrated and confirmed in the lines

of poems. Walked away with a piece
of paper said I was educated. Felt good
but I knew better. Knew a beginning
was far from an end, no way a conclusion.

3. South Bend, Golden Dome

Came upon a Golden Dome
and a Touchdown Jesus
in mosaics on the outside wall
of a library that became my home.

Met and lost one young woman
and found another in the basement
beneath the stacks where grad students
stood and scarfed hot or cold lunch

bought from vending machines
that dropped packaged food
that tasted stale and inert.
Talked books, lit crit, more books

and listened to young Dylan
and the old Delta blues, the blues
that came up to Chicago. Reborn
in the blues. Poetry in song.

Song in Beethoven, too,
in the choral movement of the Ninth.
But the poems would not begin
until the last degree was finished.

Blues came East with me,
along with a Cajun bride.
On the North Shore of an Island
off the East Coast poems came

to sing of southern Indiana woods
and hills, of hickory and walnut
and white oak and fox squirrels
and elders who spoke in German.

4. Downtown Indianapolis Townhouse

Jazz, jazz right around the corner
on the other side of the supermarket,
not far from the double gothic church
towers built for German immigrants

in this German Town part of Indy.
Jazz at the Chatterbox where
Etheridge Knight Jr. conducted
his Free People's Workshops

down the Avenue from where
he lived in the Barton Towers and I
delivered groceries for St. Vincent de Paul.
In the Chatterbox I learned to combine

poetry and jazz with a pianist-composer
who came all the way from Swabia,
on a little stage in the front corner
with a window onto Mass Avenue.

Where sixteen poets and a jazz trio
came together one Sunday night
in our favorite jazz dive to celebrate
the master who made jazz swing

in seventeen syllables and taught
us people to be free in our poems
that come of words we speak
to one another when we connect

with our idea of ancestry
that carries us beyond ourselves.
I recited E's "Poem for Myself,"
a driving blues poem that made

one woman dance when it
came out of my mouth.
And then the blues came back
into my mouth and I performed

with a man from Hammond
who slipped into Chicago
as a youth to hear the Delta guys
rip into their old and new city blues.

Who played with Yank "Mandolin Man"
Rachell here in Indy and beyond and taught
me to play some guitar and write
and play new poem-songs that came

from an old abuse by a priest
that stayed inside for fifty years
until I found the voices to speak out.
I came back home in a different way

to heal myself and others who
could not discover the right voice.
I let the boy come through
the man I became and Mr. Blues,

who rose up in me to sing
like an old friend just waiting
to help me find expression
as the shadow shuffled forth.

Indiana Prairie Fire

Joyce Brinkman (Indiana Poet Laureate 2002-2008)

Emerging color
from *silent sun*, with *beauty*
drawn from frail *grasses*

Blown *wild across* earth, fire *sounds*
crackle as *sun* surrenders

Night with prairie draped
in moon, fresh infusions loom
Autumn fire lingers

Indiana Poet Laureate Biographies

George Kalamaras (current Indiana Poet Laureate 2014 -)

George Kalamaras was born in Chicago and grew up in Cedar Lake, in Lake County, Indiana.

He has published seven books of poetry and one of scholarship including *Kingdom of Throat-Stuck Luck*, winner of the Elixir Press Poetry Contest, *The Recumbent Galaxy*, co-authored with Alvaro Cardona-Hine and winner of the C&R Press Open Competition, and *The Theory and Function of Mangoes*, winner of the Four Way Books Intro Series; seven poetry chapbooks; numerous articles in scholarly journals; and approximately 800 poems in anthologies and magazines in the United States and abroad.

His work has received numerous honors, including a Creative Writing Poetry Fellowship Grant from the National Endowment for the Arts and two Individual Artist Fellowship Grants from the Indiana Arts Commission. In 1994, he received an Indo-U.S. Advanced Research Fellowship to India. Since 1990, he has served as professor of English at Indiana University-Purdue University Fort Wayne.

Mapping the Muse

Karen Kovacik (Indiana Poet Laureate 2012 - 2014)

Karen Kovacik is a poet and translator of contemporary Polish poetry. Her books include *Metropolis Burning,* with many evocations of cities at war; *Beyond the Velvet* Curtain, winner of the Stan and Tom Wick Poetry Prize; and *Nixon and I.*

Her translation of Agnieszka Kuciak's *Distant Lands: An Anthology of Poets Who Don't Exist,* longlisted for the 2014 National Translation Award, is available from White Pine Press, and in 2016, White Pine will be publishing *Scattering the Dark: An Anthology of Polish Women Poets,* edited and selected by her.

She's Professor of English at Indiana University Purdue University Indianapolis (IUPUI), where she teaches creative writing and American poetry. Her work has been honored with the Charity Randall Citation from the International Poetry Forum, a Fulbright Research Grant to Poland, and a Fellowship in Literary Translation from the National Endowment for the Arts.

13

Norbert Krapf (Indiana Poet Laureate 2008-2010)

When **Norbert Krapf** moved from Indiana to metropolitan New York in 1970, he began to trace his family history, study German, and write poems. "Ever since then," he has written, "my passion for origins has been inseparable from my compulsion to write poems. I find it impossible to live, fully, in the present without understanding where I have lived in the past." In the poem "Tulip Poplar," the state tree of his native Indiana, he lights "the twin flames / of love and memory / of those who / came before / and disappeared / into the dark." In 2004, he moved to Indianapolis to write full time. Between his return to Indiana in 2004 and 2013, he published six collections of poetry, three with Indiana University Press, a prose memoir about childhood, and a jazz and poetry CD.

Norbert Krapf was born in 1943 in Jasper, Indiana, a German community. He graduated from Jasper High School and received a B.A. in English from St. Joseph's College, Rensselaer, IN. He received his M.A. in English from the University of Notre Dame and also his Ph.D. in English and American Literature, with a concentration in American Poetry. He taught at the C. W. Post Campus of Long Island University 1970-2004, where he is now emeritus Professor of English, was Poet Laureate 2003-2007, and directed the C. W. Post Poetry Center. He twice served in Germany as a Senior Fulbright Professor of American Poetry, at the Universities of Freiburg and Erlangen-Nuremberg. He was also a U.S. Exchange Teacher at West Oxon Technical College, England.

Joyce Brinkman (Indiana Poet Laureate 2002 - 2008)

Joyce Brinkman, Indiana Poet Laureate 2002-2008, believes in poetry as public art. She creates public poetry projects involving her poetry and the poetry of others. Collaborations with visual artists using her poetry for permanent installations include her words in a twenty- five foot stained glass window by British glass artist Martin Donlin at the Indianapolis International Airport, in lighted glass by Arlon Bayliss at the Indianapolis-Marion County Central Library and on a wall with local El Salvadoran artists in the town square of Quezaltepeque, El Salvador.

Her printed works include two chapbooks, *Tiempo Español*, and *Nine Poems In Form Nine,* and two collaborative books, *Rivers, Rails and Runways,* and *Airmail from the Airpoets* with fellow "airpoets" Ruthelen Burns, Joe Heithaus and Norbert Krapf. Joyce has received fellowships from the Mary Anderson Center for the Arts, the Arts Council of Indianapolis, and the Vermont Studio. She received a grant from the Indiana Arts Commission to explore poetry with the orangutans at the Indianapolis Zoo.

Her latest books include the multinational, multilingual book *Seasons of Sharing A Kasen Renku Collaboration*, from Leapfrog Press and *Urban Voices: 51 Poems from 51 American Poets* from San Francisco Bay Press, which she co-edited with Carolyn Kreiter-Foronda. She is a graduate of Hanover College and lives in Zionsville, Indiana, with her husband and a sweet cat.

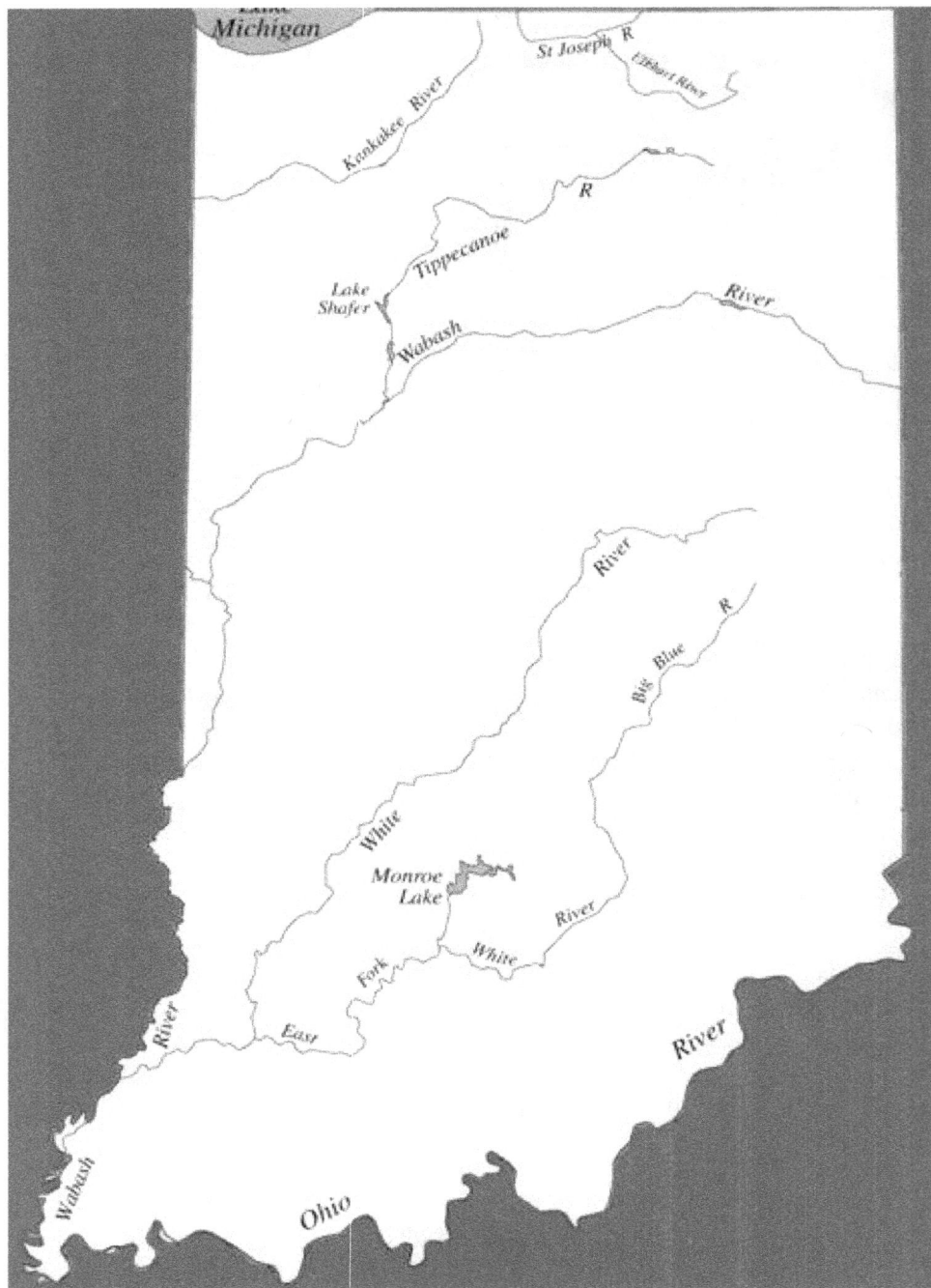

Following the Rivers' Flow

Following the Rivers' Flow: A Collaborative Poem by Joyce Brinkman, Mark Neely, Orlando Menes, Shari Wagner, Don Platt, Kevin McKelvey, Mitchell Douglas, Matthew Brennan, Marcus Wicker, Laurel Smith)

Beneath the glacial ice it flows.
Through white limestone it travels.
Not sand, nor stone can hold one long
Where water births a river.

This *one* is running out of Indiana,
Running into old associates,
Their temples white, their bodies
Growing less lacustrine every day.

Bending south, the river breaks clean
into *white* water whose rapids
Once powered mills, forges, glassworks,
but now kayaks tame its turbulence.

What the Potawatomi named for its
Elk heart *forges* past corn shocks
And wash lines, steady as a draft
Horse, slow as an Amish hymn.

The riverkeeper samples this *slow* water
To determine silt and nitrates, runoff
From farmland, holds a muddy bottle
Up to the sun so it shines in her hand.

Big Blue, were you last blue at glacial
retreat? Now, *silt* brown, nonpoint tan,
sewage gray-green, cloudy clear—or
cloudless fall sky mirrored on water.

Mapping the Muse

Wabash tither, Wapahani:
fork of east & west, concrete
to cornfield, the same *clear* soul,
current across our Hoosier spine.

Past the Dreiser Bridge, the Wabash
Widens, its wetlands pooling where
The winter crows will come, then wing
Their dark way *across* the waters.

Praise be the Ohio, hemming downtown
streets in mirrored light. *Come* forth,
tonight's widening symphony— the barge
and trains, trembling our city to sleep.

Wakeful as a new lover,
A river does not *sleep:* our dreams
In the current churn, churn. Our shared
Pulse part magic, part blood.

Prairie

Prairie: A Collaborative Poem by The Prairie Writers Guild (John D. Groppe, Pat Kopanda, Carlee Tressel Alson, Marcia Smith-Wood, Maia Hawthorne, Shannon Anderson, Doris Myers, J. Patrick Lewis, Gus Nybergm Sally Nalbor, Alyssa Cook, Connie Kingman, Joyce Brinkman)

Rensselaer, Indiana (Jasper County)

A land in need of fire
blazing life across a plain,
O Prairie, from the woodland
in splendor you emerge.

After bleak winter, longing for color
and rebirth, we wait for Shooting Stars
to rise above grasses in soft purples,
omens of honey with grasses *emerge.*

Photo Credit:

Along the fence the Spiderwort
volunteers its brilliant *color*
as I stand in silent reverie dreaming
the woods of my childhood.

Photo Credit:

19

White Beard Tongue petals whisper
trading secrets in full sun
struck *silent* only by bees
bearing tales of other blooms.

Meadows of Black-Eyed Susan!
You wild golden beauty!
May your black eyes open ours
to summer's *sun*, love, and life!

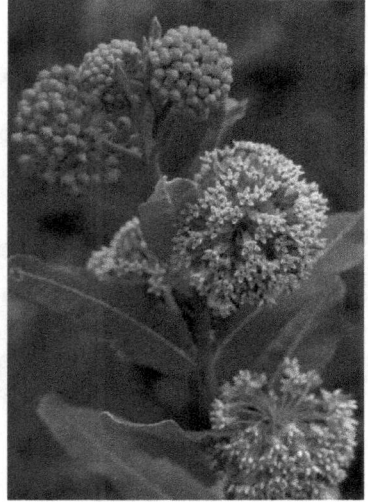

Vermilion Milkweed unfurls,
calling the *beauty*, slow and sailing,
of the butterfly, drawn irresistibly,
like tending to like.

Photo Credit:

Hagerty Ryan, U.S. Fish and Wildlife
Service / Public Domain

Amidst tall, green grasses,
sprinkles of Pale, Purple Coneflowers
delight goldfinches and their fledglings,
drawn to their prickly domes.

Photo Credit:

H. Zell / GDFL
(https://en.wikipedia.org/wiki/Wiki.Wikipedia:
Text_of_the_GNU_Free_Documentation_License)

21

Wild Bergamot, known as beebalm, stands in tall *grasses*, awaiting honeybees, sharing nectar from their tubular petals.

Photo Credit:

Immodestly named, the Blazing Star races across the prairie in *wild* abandon. In feather flower-crowns, they think they are the spires of heaven.

Photo Credit:

Mapping the Muse

Bobolink exploding in sound
rushes *across* the azure sky
descending to its mate
held in a Big Bluestem embrace.

Photo Credit:

Browsing tall Indian Grass
brushed orange 'neath languid sun,
white-tailed deer prick velvet ears
at the *sound* of whispered change.

Photo Credit:

Mapping the Muse

Along the road, Stiff Goldenrod
Shining torches among brown, dead
Stalks, for a youth 's autumn bouquet.
Bright remains of summer's setting *sun.*

Fading prairie, briefly rekindled
by fire-red Royal Catchfly petals,
signals Sandhill cranes, aloft, with
impeding evanescence of *autumn.*

Deer Mouse scurries, forages food
amid brittle bones of fallen flowers.
Fire that made the prairie burn,
beds down in winter's snow.

Indiana State Parks

Indiana State Parks: A Collaborative Poem by Indiana Federation of Poetry Clubs (Joyce Brinkman, Alice Couch, Nancy Simmonds, S. Evan Walters, Marlene Million, Alys Caviness-Gober, Jenny Kalahar, Kathy Maves, Mary Couch)

http://www.isfpc.org

Intrude in peace on life still wild!
To these living, breathing homes of wood.
To waters where the killdeer step.
Or polished sand with wind wrapped reeds.

Wander worn trails of Brown County.
Hear red-tail hawk's wings swish in flight.
Watch squirrels race about giant oaks.
Embrace *peace* beneath azure sky.

Photo Credit:

From winter riff of liquid jazz
A spring-shift to railroad thunder.
Worn fossils under Clifty Falls
Are gifts borne to the Ohio.

Photo Credit:

Mapping the Muse

The marching boots are silent now,
And *Fall* Creek whispers healing hymns
In sanctuaried life and fun...
People plying quietude.

Photo Credit:

User: Nyttend / Wikimedia Commons /
Public Domain

Winding leads where drifted dunes sprout.
Gull wings glide amid summer wind.
Bare feet sink into cool, lake sand.
Beached people pack *fun* into trips

Photo Credit:

Lori McCallister / CC-BY-2.0
(http://creativecommons.org/licenses)

26

Mapping the Muse

Along McCormick's Creek we ride,
our horses snort crisp Autumn air.
Gemstone leaves of red and yellow
gently falling through *cool* sunshine.

Photo Credit:

Chris Light / English Wikipedia / CC-BY-SA-3.0
(http://creativecommons.org/licenses)

Toboggans, magic wooden carpets
Fly through icy, *crisp* night wind
Snug cabins' welcome crackling fires
Glow till dawn's brisk Snow Lake hike

Photo Credit:

User: MrHarman / en.wikipedia / GFDL
(https://en.wikipedia.org/wiki/Wiki.Wikipedia:
Text_of_the_GNU_Free_Documentation_License)

Mapping the Muse

Springs from caves flow crisp and cool
A pioneer village from nature rose
Settlers' lives in costumed folk
Restructured memories making *magic*

Photo Credit:

User: Sjh123 / English Wikipedia /
Public Domain

Park's beginning, tulip tree home
near Sugar Creek, paddles caress
crystal waters mid sandstone runs.
Here *nature* imbues us with life.

Photo Credit:

JocalAreaNetwork / Wikimedia Commons / GFDL
(https://en.wikipedia.org/wiki/Wiki.Wikipedia:
Text_of_the_GNU_Free_Documentation_License)

Hoosier habitats for deer and frogs.
Beds of rest for sleeping bats.
Taste of paw paw, sassafras. To
Parks like swallows we return.

Back In Indiana

Robert Ummel (Allen County)

Back in Indiana two hours from its door,
back to where March Madness greets
each hardwood floor.
Basketballs are thumping, flying through the air,
each kid who played or not dreams of that final shot
and immortality there.

Back to where Booth Tarkington
and Riley penned their lines.
Penrod and Sam came to life
on pages of the Times.

Boys would go bare buttin',
Right down naked to their soul,
splishing and splashing,
in that old swimming hole.

Spring puts on a blossom show
the likes you'll never see,
And each flower gets a fix
from the buzzing of the bee

I call home — where the rivers come to greet.
That's where my kinfolk planted down their feet,
right where the St. Joseph, St. Mary's and Maumee meet.
I stand by these banks of dreams,
going back to early springs,
skinny dipping in those muddies —
bragging rights up for grabs,
seeing who would be the first to test the waters of the three,
St. Joseph, St. Mary's and the old Maumee.

It's great to be a Hoosier even when I roam.
There is no spot I'd rather be than in this place I call home.
Here basketballs are as common as raindrops in a storm,
And the next star is either here or waiting to be born.
The name to fame that stays are the heroes of the game —
hoop dreams, final shots, a mixture of Pollyanna
growing up back here in Indiana.

Heartland

Nancy Pulley (Bartholomew County)

Where the Flat Rock and the White Rivers
run chocolate with fertile earth, there are people
who don't forget the ground where they took
their first toddling steps, people glad
to be rooted in the middle of the Midwest,
to feel the pull at the end of the string
that keeps them from floating off
like lonely red balloons into the inviting fire
of an Indiana sunset. Mixed with these people
is a stunning palette of color, visitors
who decided to stay, seeds from far off lands
that blew here, settled, exotic flowers.
Together, they create buildings that write poetry
along the straight blank lines of streets.
Sculptures stand like guards,
move like dancers, reminding us of
what can come after being tempered in a hot
fire. And good music drifts over the river
at night like fog, settles in the hollows in
people's souls. Here is the maker of engines
that run the world. Here, one man's dream,
like a waterfall, can collect other dreams,
carry them down to the White River, take them
to the Mississippi. They run through the country
like blood, reminding others of the heart that
pumps, the land that grows the corn that
feeds the stomach, the thrumming, beating heartland.

Benton County Sunsets

Maddie Weimer (Benton County)

Past the sharp edges of the subdued wire fence,
Cascading lower over the compact coffee-colored Montmorenci rooftops,
The Crimson Lover paints mountains
above the small white church beside the cemetery.
Purple blazes through apparitions of swirling soaring spires
Whilst musical birds bid farewell into rising silence
And the rare red-headed woodpecker finishes his pecking.
The Ruling Light ushers dimming snug kisses to
Her rowdy dogs, whispering corn fields, and tireless workers of hardened hands.
The grasses wave softly with the wind toward Otterbein,
Pursuing the last drops of honey rays, jealous of the quiet town.
She allows herself to fall until she ceases to display her radiance,
And so the Greater Light succumbs to the Lesser once again.

Boone's Pillars of Legacy

Brenda Miller (Boone County)

"Tooott-ooott!"
The whistle signals not any common train.
Special Delivery!
Laborers and citizens gather
For the unloading.
Flatbed cars held under chain
Immense blocks of Hoosier limestone.
A lathe to turn not yet invented,
Masons began their opus.
From many hands, many hours
Emerged polished round pillars.
Raised to straddle the state's meridian line,
Over thirty-five feet of single-piece Booneite glory,
The columns are a triumph unrivaled.
Two pairs face North, two pairs South,
The Courthouse has no peer.

A Song of Brown County

Keith Bradway (Brown County)

Come sing a song of this fair land
Or strum it with a bluegrass band
Of Clupper's grove and Bill Monroe
Resplendent at his springtime show.

That man who cut your silhouette
While puffing on his cigarette.
Frank Hohenberger's photographs
Of liar's benchers; hear their laughs.

Kin Hubbard's written tapestry
Of county folk with sophistry.
Where T.C. Steele the portraitist
Made paintings of the morning mist.

A picnic spot, a shady nook,
Bean Blossom and its overlook.
The wooded hills in summer haze,
The park in autumn all ablaze.

Its ponds and lakes in summer fair
Whose waters fishermen may dare.
For streamlets which inspire our thanks
With sycamores along their banks.

Of sassafras and whip-poor-wills,
Persimmon trees and sorghum mills,
Contentedness of evening hush
And clear tones of the woodland thrush.

Come sing a song of Brown County;
Of heavenly hills and home.

At Adams' Mill

Christian Knoeller (Carroll County)

To build this mill Adams divined
how gravity would have its way
with water between these hills

hiked fifty miles of Wildcat Creek
to find the right hollow, imagined
a dam upstream of the oxbow

to drive the turbine and huge
grindstones enshrined today
by the roadside. Water

surges down the raceway
in the wake of August rains
with the same force that turned

half the county's corn to flour
for a hundred summers.
The mill's a self-proclaimed

Museum of Americana now,
four stories of wooden hayforks
and rakes, great blades

that harvest only nostalgia
these days. The river sluices
through the foundation fifty

feet below powering
wooden wheels with nothing
left to

Make Use

Marissa Rose (Delaware County)

Geese part like lips above the foundry ruins
where fifty years ago, strong-backed men

stooped over tremendous crucibles,
pounding metal castings out of earthen ore

that wanted no direction. Like the coffee table
where my mother rests her glass bowl of oranges:

two planks from a dead barn that once stood
a mile from here, stripped down to the grain

so its knotted eye of oak wakes and blinks
with restored vision. Like the plastic daffodils

blown off last year's Easter wreath, replanted
in my neighbor's late-winter window box:

their palm-shaped faces still earnestly, beyond
what is reasonable, in praise of yellow.

That's what we do where I live: we make use.
Even the geese circle down when they tire

of the atmosphere, the rusted slabs of ironware
bearing the flock's flitting, winged revelry

like a new playground, built over a surface
that never holds one shape for long:

beneath the fresh-stirred dust is a molten core,
bubbling with atoms fit for rearrangement.

Survivor's Prayer

Linda E. Reschly Schrock (Elkhart County)

God, make it go away!
This awful black thing that snakes and bulges, turns and twists
It dangles from the sky like a noose. Then it snaps up and cuts off, sucks out and spits up
      The possessions we hold close and value.
Those expressions of our private hopes and dreams; beliefs and achievements
      Become public, mixed together, defiled, invaded and discarded
      Like meaningless garbage to be gawked at, walked on, destroyed, burned.
And in our vulnerable mixed up ambivalence here come those who are concerned or curious
      Nosy and invasive, newsy or supportive, helpful and sharing
If only they wore hats to fit their role. If only they played only one role!

In our confused vulnerability it's hard to know who we are and what we need.
How can we deal with another's complexity when our own needs are so overwhelming?

Yes, the damaging funnel is gone.
Make the pain, ambivalence, depression, despair and fear go away.
Show us the security and nourishment of Your love through the actions of others who help
      And do not invade the solitude and privacy of our pain by driving by and gawking,
      Flying over and circling, peeping through viewfinders.
In our joy of survival help us show Your love to those whose loved ones did not survive.

There were deaths from this storm. Why? They followed the rules.
      They were no better, no worse than anyone else.
The relief of our friends in our survival was wonderful, appreciated, needed.
      So why did You take these friends?
      Okay, so You didn't take these friends. But why them?

Is that why I'm angry? Do I wonder how a God who loves me, supports me, protects me
      Could not or would not intervene with love, support and protection for these friends
      Will You not intervene for me, for my loved ones?

My head can deal with this. My heart can't deal with the grief I feel
      For my friends, for my loss of security that my family will be safe when I come home.
      That my possessions will be undisturbed by weather beyond my control
      That my privacy will not be invaded by people driving by and gawking
While I gather up another's trash or treasure, and not be able to decide which it is.

I go on living, as do others. Workers can help bring the buildings back.
      Its life I can't deal with now. Bring me back to happiness, security, love and life.
God, I need You to make this go away and bring life back to my survival.

More to See

Doug Easley (Fayette County)

Although Connersville was platted in 1813,
there is more of its history to see.
Let us look back to 1808, and make a mental note.
In the beginning, John Conner and family first arrived on a boat.
Conner searched for a place to move his family's trading post,
a trading post that traded furs for the very most.
The West Fork of the White River carried them to this twelve mile site.
Conner soon had a bigger vision within his sight.
Having visions of settlers who would come in time,
Conner made the "Twelve Mile Purchase" of 1809.
Sixty-two lots were platted that day.
Soon after construction was underway.
Please don't forget Michael Peltier.
He was Conner's partner, down at the trading post there.
Population created more changes as it grew.
This pleased the settlers when the canal came through.
The canal provided much of what was needed.
It provided seeds for planting, and even flour women kneaded.
As demands for goods and services grew,
the town developed a need for the railroad in 1862.
Connersville does have a lot of history to share.
This can be seen just about everywhere.
Look at the Fayette County Free Fair.
Livestock, food, and even quilts, as one may know,
can be found displayed at the 4-H show.
Both adults and children win ribbons, trophies and certificates too.
The Fayette County Free Fair 4-H winners are part of history too.
Let us not forget the Free Fair Queen who is picked every year,
for at the Free Fair parade she causes the crowds to cheer.
Or one may just take a walk,
noticing the history in Roberts Park.
"Roberts" was the name of the man
who originally owned the land.
One would have to note the covered bridge sitting there.
It is a piece of history that Connersville is proud to share.
Although there is so much more to see
about Connersville's history.
Please keep in mind Connersville began its time
through vision, hard work, and families like yours and mine.

Fountain County's Pride

F.A. Vickery (Fountain County)

We're not a hub for politics
Or top of the social mountain,
But we've got a lot to be proud of
In this county we call Fountain.

Famous men have called this home:
Lew Wallace and George D. Hayes.
Lew studied law and led the troops
For the Union in Civil War days.

George had a different kind of dream,
To reach the world with song.
He'd start the Grand Ole Opry
And keep it going strong.

The courthouse walls have murals grand
of our history we love to share.
From the brush of Eugene Savage,
There is no place that can compare.

General Shoup was soon to run West Point
Under President Kennedy.
His troops fought in battle, died in war,
Defending our land from tyranny.

Many tons of oak and fine hard wood,
Each year are dried and sawed.
We made the bricks for a world-class track.
The "Five Hundred" now it's called.

We made things of steel in olden days
For cars and trains and dozers.
And we still do make parts from steel
To ship the whole world over.

Mapping the Muse

We quarried stone for railroad lines
That made the nation grow.
And coal to feed those very trains
A long, long time ago.

Please, don't forget the things we grow.
That's corn and beans and wheat.
And add to that our apple crops,
So crunchy, round, and sweet.

The folks are good and kind and brave
In this county we call Fountain.
In this land of rolling hills and plains,
Industry's our only mountain.

Home

Claire Eckstein (Franklin County)

The rich soil
Moaning machinery
Our rattling ancestors bones

A fresh breeze
Holds us up
Accepting and warm

The skies, so blue
The pastures, always green
The families, forever loving

Tractor shows and pulls
Fairs and fests
Never far from us

This is our home
Where we are growing
Flourishing
And readying for harvest

Our Town

Marie Julian (Gibson County)

A squirrel found an acorn
And put it away you see.
He left it in the ground,
Then we had a huge oak tree.

That huge oak tree had acorns.
They fell all around.
Wind and snow and people
Pushed them into the ground.

The trees came up all over.
There was a huge forest of oaks.
People who came to see them
Said, "What a pleasant place for folks."

They planted their desires it seems
Like the acorns in the ground.
The village grew as in their dreams,
And they called it Oakland Town.

They had so many oak trees;
They thought it was a pity.
They cut the trees to build you see,
Now they call it Oakland City.

Along the Mississinewa

Dan Fuller (Grant County)

Scattering leaves underfoot,
I stroll along the Mississinewa River,
Watching the water flow slowly by,
As it has done every day,
For a thousand years...and more.

An Indian village stood near here once,
In morning haze, smoke seems to rise, from the blaze of bygone fires,
When buckskinned braves banked their canoes,
As their raven-haired wives stir pots of beans and corn and squash,
Crooning softly harvest songs to their brown-skinned babes.

Some two hundred years ago
They fought a battle against soldiers
Who did not understand
That we are all children
of the same Great Father.

They're gone now.
Indians and soldiers.
Re-enactors come yearly
To portray their parts.
The forest rings again
With war whoops and musket fire,
But the re-enactors have left, too,
Packed up and dissipated into the present.

It's all peaceful today.
The only war paint on leaves,
Drifting down to the river's surface,
Forming colorful flotillas,
Sailing silently toward the sea.

Mapping the Muse

The only sound is the cheep
Of a chickadee,
A squirrel rustling leaves,
Or is that a moccasin-clad footstep?

Today I walk with ghosts,
of memories for centuries silent,
In the dappled leaf light,
I hear them whisper,
We were here... We were here,
Now... We rest,
Along the Mississinewa.

An Old Covered Bridge in Greene County

Carol Ogdon (Greene County)

There's a covered bridge all weathered and worn
that must have some stories to tell;
the Richland Creek runs under it
and the Plummer Creek as well.

The bridge was built by the Kennedys
in eighteen-and-eighty-three;
just think of the water that's gone under the bridge
and all of its history.

I'm sure there were folks with a horse and buggy
found shelter from the rain;
and some who drove Models T's through there
or pulled a wagon of grain.

It might have been a meeting place
for children and couples in love,
who secretly left their notes inside
while birds roosted in rafters above.

Repairs have been made to restore the bridge
now new memories become a part
of the dates and names carved on these walls—
sweet memories carved in our heart.

County Fair

Stephen R. Roberts (Hamilton County)

The trouble seemed to be Bertha Bonap
tripped over the aisle broom, banged her knee
on a hog trough and screamed bloody murder.

Old man Comer, unsteady legs twisted
from a combine accident a decade back,
bent over to help upright the old girl,
lost his balance and ended up contorted
into a what quickly came to be referred to
as an awkwardly compromised position.

Preacher Barrel Snook heard tell of the rumor
and climbed up a pile of horse dung in back
of the riding rink in his endless search for sinners.
He commenced to punch at his worn good book
with an emphatic fist as he cast Bible verses
over the grounds like fairy dust or herbicide.

This all took place as the winner of the contest
for pork queen climbed to the stage to salute family,
friends, and a few animals of her homestead barnyard.
The new and nervous squeal-queen in her iced crown
couldn't help but hear Preacher Snook yodeling of sin,
which caused her to drop her smile and defenses.

She forgot her two paragraph speech, getting confused
between what was happening under starlight tonight,
and what had taken place the night before
with Bradley Bonap – Bertha's awesome nephew -
in the straw-padded bed of his customized Chevy pickup,
parked out back in the deep shadows of the sheep barn.

So she broke down and started confessing.
This perked up the crowd a bit, got them to talking
about current affairs, what the world's come to,
and that the only decent things left are church,
chocolate ice cream, and that new reality show
just started on sixteen, right after the news and weather.

45

West Siders

Stacy Post (Hendricks County)

Hendricks County is...
a crane's flight from the Capitol,
a butterfly's breath from concrete canals
and sports stadiums,
mere miles from top museums.

To scuttle to city work
is to drive with sun in your eyes
to strive for that middling American dream.
To journey home again
is to drive with sun in your eyes,

always squinting,
during the congested evening hour
heading home to combed
tamed fields turned
into subdivisions.

Hendricks County is...
home to transplants and old timers,
farms and fields,
churches and libraries,
strip malls and chain stores.

Westsiders hustle
and huddle—
the bustle of daily life
providing convenient
communal light.

As For Me, Give Me Henry County

Robert Stephen Dicken (Henry County)

Summer across the Hoosier heartland:
Summit Lake and Westwood Lake awash with fishermen,
Memorial Park teeming with ants and picnickers,
I sit in the shade under the raintree on a sunny day
And listen to the sweet corn grow on a humid night,
In these lands of spice, creeks of honey, springs of sulfur.

Fall across the Hoosier heartland:
A fiery palette of dying leaves spans the Cadis horizon.
School buses, getting their acts together and taking them on the roads,
Snake through the harvesting acres.
On the way to Hickory, they pass sleepy combines,
Their headlights peering through swirling clouds of dust.

Winter across the Hoosier heartland:
Dairy cattle ruminate in warm, straw-filled Straughn barns
And their masters ruminate in cozy, historic homesteads.
Howling winds and blinding snows rage outside
While curious students read Beard and Heller inside,
Writing their school reports on Wright, Grose, and Bundy.

Spring across the Hoosier heartland:
Farmers turn the potent black loam,
Planting their hopeful soybeans and corn.
The potent, black Kennard sky portends the danger of twisters.
March proclaims the hysteria of Bobcats and Cossacks,
And even the Hall enshrines Alford, Benson, Pavy, and Pierce.

In all seasons, give me Henry County,
Home to many, wherever they might live.
In their hearts, they carry the honest values of the heartland.
In their memories, they carry the players who filled the stage.
Meanwhile, the courthouse of Lockridge embraces the LOVE of Indiana

And Indiana smiles, Indiana celebrates.

Howard County: Home To My Heart

Lisa Fipps (Howard County)

My heart's home is Howard County, where lifelong memories abound.

I remember when I was a child ...
Picking dandelion bouquets for Mom,
leaving my hands stained and stinking of an earthy scent.
Chasing flickering lightning bugs to put in Ball jars, nature's nightlight by my bed.
Showing off Old Ben and the Sycamore Stump to visiting out-of-town relatives.
Playing in the parks after picnics,
pumping my legs on the swings to go higher, higher, and higher still.
Biting into red, ripe, round tomatoes fresh off the vine,
feeling juice flow down my chin.
Finding faith to fill and refill me when the world takes, takes, takes.
Camping along the Wildcat,
setting sweet, sticky marshmallows aflame over a crackling smoky fire.
Picking out pumpkins, meandering through corn mazes, bundling up on hayrides,
and sipping fresh apple cider in autumn.
Praying for snowstorms, ear to the radio waiting for those two magical words: snow day.
Sledding and building snowmen before helping stir together
some snow cream so I could lick the spoon.

I remember when I was a teenager ...
Swimming at the Seashore and, later, basking in the sun at Kokomo Beach.
Learning from teachers who became lifelong mentors.
Sweating while detasseling tall skin-slicing stalks of corn in the humid Hoosier heat.
Watching fireworks light up the sky over the courthouse square.
Red. White. Blue. Boom! Sparkle! Fizzle.
Celebrating our history and heritage during downtown parades and festivals.
Catching up with classmates near the whirling lights,
spun sugar cotton candy, and fried fare at the fair.
Cheering on the home team at basketball games,
squeaking shoes on the shiny court, swooshing nets, buzzing scoreboards –
Hoosier hysteria!

I remember as an adult ...
Bragging at college about my town being the home to America's first automobile,
a first of many.
Meeting friends over a meal and savoring every morsel
of the conversation along with the food.
Being in awe of how much our community gives whenever there's a need.
Realizing how special Howard County is when you're far away,
thinking you've outgrown it.
Wishing to turn back the clock to the simple days
of fluttering curtains covering open windows
welcoming cool night breezes, cricket music, and the who-whoing of horned owls.

Howard County,
a place you can always come back to,
a place with welcome arms,
a place to call home – if not by address than at least by your heart.

I'm a Proud Huntington Hoosier

Rosella Corll (Huntington County)

I'm a proud Huntington Hoosier.
I have lived here ninety-one years.
I've had a wonderful life
Including, laughter, fun, and tears.

I've never lived on a farm but I know,
Rural life-style rubbed off on me.
The country seems to create great folks
I believe like them, we should be.

The Huntington County families
For the most part are kind and good.
They're willing to help each other,
As they promised they always would.

If they are rich or if they're not,
They are generous and willing to share.
Generosity shows their loving hearts
And I know they will always care.

Our County has many fine churches.
Great teachers in high-rated schools.
Our strong leaders govern important jobs,
We acknowledge their well-planned rules.

Our Hospital is the very best.
Huntington University is our jewel.
Students there have earned and received
A great educational tool.

We celebrate, also enjoy
Parades with floats and bands.
We've many sport teams we truly support.
We've become their local fans.

Mapping the Muse

We have parks and walking trails.
Several lakes to enjoy with our boat.
Go to the 'Forks of the Wabash'
It's a historic place you will note.

Children look for something to do.
Activities they'd like to try.
They join 'Boys and Girls' club with their friends.
There's sports at the 'Pal' and the 'Y'.

One may travel our land or abroad
But where ever you may roam,
You'll find no better, peaceful place
Than Huntington County, we call "Home".

For Julia Howland Healey, With Gratitude

Carlee Tressel Alson (Jasper County)

How do we remember a woman
whose life mattered
in the way that all lives matter—
in the receiving of each day
and the going where life will go?

We look to what she wrote
of herself
of Perrysburg and Logansport
and Rensselaer—
the place that would always be home.

For her there was no end
to the books to read,
and ideas to think,
though she held the wisdom of Lincoln
above them all.

Such praises she gave a man
so plain in his speech
so profound in thought—
a man she called
the greatest the world has ever known.

For me, Mrs. Healey,
the greatness was in you
for you marked the path with words—
those weathered and tumbled stones,
the ones we leave for each other
to notice,
to pick up and ponder,
to hold for a moment
and feel.

[Mrs. Julia Howland Healey lived from February 9, 1840, to May 14, 1913. She composed her own obituary and published with it was an article she wrote about Abraham Lincoln. Mrs. Healey is buried in Weston Cemetery in Rensselaer.] .

Jay County, Indiana, 2016

Mable Jean Caylor (Jay County)

The climate that's here in mild summer time
Causes soybeans and corn to reach their prime;
And the roots reach down to moisture there
To nourish if a drought comes, unaware.

The wheat grows ripe with its heavy bronze heads
To help feed the world with life-saving breads.

The white concrete arch of our historic bridge
Is part of our 100-year heritage.

The Antique Tractor and Gas Engine Show (in August)
is the world's largest, now 50 years or so.

Our courthouse in Portland was built in 1916 of Bedford
Stone & marble with 104 windows. What sets it apart is the
beautiful historic paintings covering the dome, overhead.

In 1910, Elwood Haynes, a local man
Invented the horseless carriage, his plan.
There is a large mural of him and his car
On a brick wall. Look for it-Meridian & West Arch-
not far

We've those who eat veggies they've raised themselves,
With pickles and jellies on pantry shelves
Gardens and flowers are not all one sees
With humming birds, monarchs and bumble bees.

The 4-H kids win ribbons at the Jay County Fair
There are horse racing and other programs there.

Our neighbors "pitch in" if there is a need,
To work together to help us succeed.
It is a fact that we'll never roam, as
JAY COUNTY, INDIANA, IS OUR HOME, SWEET HOME!

Watershed

Kay Stokes (Jefferson County)

After they douse the courthouse,
the golden dome gone to ribs and tatters,
they lie down in their gear
on the sidewalk,
neat as railroad ties
helmets still at hand
ready for a spark in the night,
the great skeleton steaming
above them.

All night, the water rolls
down Jefferson Street.
Overflowing limestone gutters,
sheeting across pavement,
down and down
in cascades and torrents,
down to the river
where the settlers
came ashore.

Farmers and card sharps
storekeepers and cattlemen
headed up the Michigan Road,
wagons filled with grit
and provisions. In the hollows,
the underground conducted
a more tender business.
Swimmers waded in,
the South at their backs.
Freighted into Georgetown,
They alighted for a night
in hollow chimneys.
At Neil's Creek
lanterns burned bright
along the ridges.

The great plume of ash wafts
over farms and creeks and woods,
the land a rippled quilt
cut from Indian country.
From Hanover and Chelsea,
Canaan and Manville,
they descend the hills,
gather, gawk, sob
in the streets,
neighbors and strangers
come for witness
and companionship.

The sidewalk sleepers
wake at dawn,
swaddled in rubber and canvas.
Two hundred volunteers,
there not for pay
but for provenance.
They rise, cramped,
chilly from the concrete,
carry out sodden plats,
deeds in careful copperplate,
testaments of great-grandparents,
hundred-year-old marriage records
giving license to their futures.

These pioneers stitched
the Ohio to the uplands
with the first locomotives,
trained missionaries
for the Territories.
Fed and clothed
and put the starch
in the Midwest,
braced the world's saddles,
wrought its iron spines,
made its bacon, buttoned
its trousers and dresses.

Mapping the Muse

Settled the union
then helped save it,
a third of the county
off to war, then home
by steamer, above decks
or below them.
Two hundred years of flooding creeks
and scrapbooks blown to Ohio,
economies gone dead as Gettysburg,
missed embers, bodies
docking in the bellies of boats.
History's a tinder business
This is our third courthouse.
We are old hands
at wind and flame
and restoration.

So we flash freeze the past.
Maps and plats packed
into cryotrucks,
pulled into vacuum,
water driven to vapor,
back to the sky.
Ancient pages returning
crisp as wedding invitations
barely a year later.

Because, after all,
it's the 21st century.
And the courthouse?
We dry it out,
build it back again.

Jennings County – Land of Winding Waters
Jennifer Rockhold (Jennings County)

Hundreds of millions of years ago beneath a shallow sea,
Ancient jawless fishes swam and crinoids danced,
Primitive creatures of the sea destined to live, to die, and to calcify.
Blue North Vernon limestone would be born of these primeval waters
For the future roads and bridges of Jennings County.

Ten thousand years ago, glaciers scoured out the Great Lakes,
Leveled northern Indiana and advanced southward,
Buckling the earth's crust and depositing boulders and sediment.
Southeastern Indiana's newly undulating landscape then
Slept and awaited earth's eventual warming.

Glacial Ice Age water became rivulets and the rivulets became larger streams
Which transformed into the creeks and rivers of Jennings County
Destined to wind through hard karst in search of the great Ohio Valley.
Natives named the largest of these "Mus-Cat-A-Tuk" or "Winding Waters",
Another, "Laque-Ka-Ou-E-Nek" or "Water Running Through Sand".

Where rich alluvial bottoms formed native peoples lived, planted, fished,
Chipped flint from rock walls exposed by corrosive waters,
Buried their loved ones in stone mounds on bluffs.
Obscured today by oak and poplar forests, ancient cemeteries lie hidden.
Only hawks and ancestral spirits watch over them now.

Natives gathered large creek stones, stained them with walnut and bloodroot,
Scorched and blackened them in ceremonial fires,
Upon them laid animal bones, cakes of maize, and mussel shells.
Unaware of the past that would lay beneath them as they slept,
Settlers moved in and founded homesteads upon them instead.

White men had come in great numbers to build grist and woolen mills,
Ingenious swinging bridges of wire and wood to span treacherous waters,
And quarry the blue North Vernon limestone for bridge abutments.
They had come to preach and to pray in simple white churches
And bury their dead in uniformly numbered lots in town.

Mapping the Muse

Above a winding bend in Sand Creek near the bustling village of Brewersville
Lay a white giant and small child within a stone mound on Mr. Robison's farm.
Adorned ceremoniously with necklace of mica and burnt spring of cedar,
The legendary 9'8' giant of Brewersville was disinterred in 1884.
State geologists and archaeologists were astounded.

Kept in a basket at Kellar's mill and played with by local children,
The bones were unceremoniously swept downstream in a flood in 1939.
Do mussel shells adorn them now on Sand Creek's sandy bottom?
Might they dwell beneath tangled wire from a fallen swinging bridge?
Both bones and time appear forever lost in Jennings County's winding waters.

The Magic of Small Town Living

Mya Holbrook (Johnson County)

It is difficult for some to see it's appeal,
like an old oak table, it's stain-faded after generations
of enthusiastic use and sentimentality,
beneath each blemish and scratch, a story.
Their implications indecipherable to all but a few.

Teenagers in our hometown
march closer to their high school diplomas
with every intention of breaking away,
and making plans that leave little room for
Christmases spent with their grandparents
or kids of their own.

They dream of big cities full of public transportation,
      and cardboard box apartments that don't allow pets
        for fear they would ruin the carpet.

Smog flavored sunsets
and offhanded conversations about the weather,
or the traffic in the city that day must make for a lonely way of life.

At night, I look up at the sky, mottled with clouds,
traveling low against the canvas of a full moon.

There, I am comforted not
from the distant glow of faint sparkling stars,
      or beautiful cities gleaming always just on the horizon
but from the blipping red light
of a telephone tower,
reminding me that I am home.

It's hard to accept that not everyone
can see themselves reflected in cracked sidewalks
and old country roads.

Mapping the Muse

Childhood friends and training wheels
never had a chance to populate a family photo album,
To those without the privilege of growing up in a small town,
Old tables are only old tables.
Blinking tower lights don't rattle their ribcages
like a second internalized heartbeat.

Town and Country Medley

Laurel Smith (Knox County)

1. *Welcome*

Tribal chiefs, pilgrims,
        families have stopped here in times
        before market days
or July parades. Lincoln
himself was once a stranger.

2. *Outboard tour*

Imagine, he says,
        the river as highway, main
street. Everything from
fish to fresh pearls. Muddy? Sure,
        but it shines in the moonlight.

3. *Seasonal fare*

Wild asparagus
strawberries, lettuce, chard.
        Tomatoes, green beans
apples, peaches, yellow squash,
        and melon, melon, melon.

4. *On occasion*

Dancing in the streets:
        the children start, happy on
their feet. Soon we join,
convinced that our awkward steps
        will be forgiven at dusk.

5. *Monument*

Marble rotunda,
        pillars of granite, painted
        history portrayed
on these walls: almost as grand
as the Wabash, flowing still.

Royer Lake, La Grange County, Indiana

Carol Massat (La Grange County)

It is September.
Three deer step out into the lake each day,
Browsing and quiet in the still waters, morning and evening.
Boats pause and stop and watch until, with a flick of the tail, each deer leaps into the
darkened woods.

On the other side of the lake,
In the third cottage, a woman wears scarves and fights breast cancer.
At the end of the road,
a mother hugs her 32 year old daughter who can speak only with
this language of the body:
smiles, hugs, laughter, tears, a muteness louder than the deer
On the other side of the lake.

On the Gulf, hurricanes and prayers fill the skies,
But here it is September. The deer pace the shallows.
A blue heron pauses and then flies to the other side of the lake.
Within the waters, life rises to the surface and dives deep again
On the underside of the lake.

The sun rises over the waters.
The Milky Way emerges in the sacred night.
In the deepest darkness
There is light.

All Washed Up

Jackie Huppenthal (Lake County)

Driftwood
skipping stones
seagull feathers

beach glass
assorted shells
great lake treasures

Our sand castle
was well adorned
with items from the deep

borrowed gifts
reclaimed too soon
swept from you and me

The Magic of Autumn

Dondeena Caldwell (Madison County)

Autumn: *chanson triste,*
spider-fingered notes
weaving tonal webs in filigree,
dew-studded duets.

Melancholy music
from beads of blackbirds
strung on abacus telephone wires,
cawing summer's dirge.

Melodies, mist-muffled,
of cloud-shrouded wind
softly rustling dry arpeggios
on cornstalk keyboards.

Interlude at harvest,
 bittersweet refrain
in gold over gloom
as summer sings amen.

Poetry Fountain

Richard Pflum (Marion County)

It sprouts needles, stinging in all directions, the water
circumnavigating our dimensions. We are surprised
to see these little crystalline dollops gamboling about
in infrared-toward-ultraviolet, in their string tied
rainy-coats and drenched bikinis. They let viewers
peek through every now and then as they play their
fabulous overtones on polysyllabic flutes, harps
and cymbals before allowing a metaphoric piano to
introduce Stradivari strings with their wooden bow ties
and aromatic scent of pine resin behind each ear.

For the waters are extravagant notes quavered
to rhythms of triangles and silver toned drums;
are plays of light in the afternoon lull of acoustic
clouds floating high between Arcturus and Vega.
Ah this fountain! Playing only for odds-and-ends
we find between toes in our tight fitting shoes
or what is in half-filled pockets now stuffed with
soiled tissues and grandfather clocks.

Still we enjoy it – here in this plebian park where
pedestrians sit in a wistful-restful, autumnal haze after
lunch, dreaming the restored bodies of Pan and his
voluptuous, virginal, Nymph, enriched now in their new
bronze cures to a rich green patina, covering an ancient
thievery's scars as our liquid Muse continues to sing.

Miami County Indiana

Norma Wideman (Miami County)

Miami County as well as our country was created by God and organized by man.
Who lived and died for those now and in the future who took a stand.
For our county like many others will always have struggles.
We grieve, for every father, mother, son and daughter.
That went off on land, air or water.
To unknown lands they go.
For a county and country that is worth the fight.
We unite hand in hand across this nation.
From every city, town and farm we are one amazing creation.
It isn't always easy but well worth it.
The sense of pride is overwhelming as we look around now and in the past.
For those who were brave enough to do what was right.
You fight the fight.
I salute you.

Heading Home

Leah Helen May (Monroe County)

End of the day in the flat lands
north of my home county.
A peach-blow sunset,
bands of apricot and rose stretch
on the wide, flat horizon.
This glaciated land is strange to me
with its broad acres and endless fields
of corn and soybeans.
After the glaciers melted this must have been
a flat wetland of rushes and cat-tails
that became black, peaty soil.

I am from hilly limestone land;
Monroe County, with its little fields,
its forests and deep-cutting streams,
its gray bluffs with their patina
of ferns and wild hydrangeas....
No grinding fields of ice have scraped it smooth.
Time and the soft knives of running water
scored it into hills, ravines and hollows.
It is creased and wrinkled
like the face of a handsome old woman.

I'm Writing You A Postcard

Gerburg Garmann (Montgomery County)

A platform from which to begin:
a worn carpet, a sturdy old bed with some cat scratches,
a soft layer of blankets to be peeled away with the seasons
or settled back one over the other to furnish warm pockets of air,
two open windows letting in birdsong from the wet summer garden,
a rounded desk conforming to the curves of a woman's body,
orange curtains sheer with light allowing for gaps between words
before they decamp again.
That's when the paintings on the latte colored walls arrange you
in music and make you wonder who spoke them or sang them before
they spoke to you and edited your sound.
Inexpensive shadows, limping rain:
The air breathes itself in hiccups,
time masquerades as time, and the teakettle
does not stop whistling.
Feathers light as silk contemplate an outcropping of awkwardness
in the not so distant sky, scissors tire of paper, and solitude comes
out of nowhere, almost too easy to lift.
That's what air embracing air must feel like.
I am writing you a postcard filled with seasons and latte colored music
that whistles raindrops carried on feathers as light as silk.

Morgan's Resolutions

Kelly McNeil (Morgan County)

O Morgan General make your stand
We place your name upon our land
Fierce and true of noble cause
Of your life you gave no pause.

Southern Quakers took their stand
Opposed to slav'ry in their land
Flocking here to land of free
Fight prejudice, man's enemy

Watercourse, a trail to blaze
Beckoning soul to stand and gaze
White River, a clear divide
Abundant life on either side

Furrowed brow and furrowed land
With farmer heart and calloused hand
Straight the course and eye that's true
Land produced and strength renew

Cataract from down below
Artesian well forever flow
Bring your life add to the mix
Minerals organic matrix

Brush to hold a watered hue
With blazing gold and sacred blue
Banner waves in Indiana!
For Crossroads of America

Bucket brigades, fish to world
Our caring arms remain unfurled
Those close and far need to breathe
Pray find our love remains unsheathed

Mapping the Muse

Lift your head O Gateway South
Praise and good to fill your mouth
Open wide and seek to share
Cast off the locks and chains you hear

Run to future hope in heart
Community to do our part
Many days have laid to rest
But forward lies the best of best

Undue scorn and shame of sin
You've weathered storms without, within
Let God shed his grace on thee
Be blessed and whole, Morgan County

Sweet Valley

John Lyttle (Owen County)

Roll down the hill
toward the river

Lift up your eyes
to a cold star-bright sky

Breathe in the scent
of welcoming wood smoke

And watch mist swirl
over the water

See the valley
pull clouds down to its bosom

Celebrate this valley
Home to the stone-knapper,
The fur trader, the root buyer.

This is our home, our valley
Our sweet valley

Parke County Autumn

Joan Lunsford (Parke County)

As cool air embraces the warm waters
Of Raccoon Creek to form a morning mist,
A fog that hovers lightly through the dawn,
The covered bridges lie o'er winding streams
Like ancient dinosaurs that groan beneath
The passage of one million visitors.

A brisk wind rattles fragile cornstalks
In one last standing ovation for Fall.
Bronzed fields of soybeans have dropped their leaves
To offer ripened pods of golden seed
As monstrous combines crawl across the fields
Like giant anteaters to harvest grain.

The hollyhocks have shed their final blooms
With next year's seed dispersed into the soil,
While hummingbirds have hummed their last good-bye
And headed south in heed of nature's call.
Summer's repertoire is now complete,
Replaced with pumpkins, bittersweet, and mums.

The trees explode in oranges, yellows, reds
Of maple, cherry, sassafras, and oak.
We're blessed each year with Autumn's vibrant hues;
Its fleeting beauty lingers in our souls.
A haven from the burden of life's toil
With grateful hearts we claim this spot as home.

Tears Came Falling Down From Heaven

Joan Goble's 2010 Cannelton Elementary 5ᵗʰ Grade Class (Perry County)

It's still winter here at this peaceful place,
As rain falls gently
Like tears falling down from heaven
Let us remember when . . .

It happened one March day
The 17ᵗʰ in the year 1960,
When tears came falling down from Heaven
There was loss a plenty.

Sixty-three souls together
Came to this solemn place,
And tears came falling down from Heaven
Like raindrops down a face.

Where did they come from?
Does anyone know?
The tears who came falling down from Heaven
On this silent field of snow.

Their origins were many,
Their futures were so bright,
These tears falling down from Heaven
It just doesn't seem quite right.

This place was quiet and restful
We couldn't understand
When tears came falling down from Heaven
Quite peaceful was the land.

Heavy were the hearts
of the people who came to help,
Their tears came falling down from Heaven
Such sorrow that overwhelmed.

For there was no one they could aid
Not a soul was there in sight,
As tears came falling down from Heaven
No way to help their plight.

All of Perry County came together
With love, sympathy, and comfort
When tears came falling down from Heaven
All helped in any way they could.

Those sixty-three innocent souls
Who came to rest at this peaceful place,
Those tears that came falling down from Heaven
Our minds will not erase.

Their spirits live on and on,
Lifting off the clouds of sadness today,
No longer tears falling down from Heaven
They give us hope for each new day.

Here we have a memorial to remember
Each man, woman, and child —don't fret,
Now they all dwell in beautiful Heaven
And we will never, ever forget!

Thoughts and Memories of this Region

Ryan Fredric Steinbeck (Porter County)

We are crossing patterns.
From this dune I look out across the lake.
I am one with sunrise,
As birds play on the rocky beach,
The acetylene from steel mills carries heavy in the air,
This view never tires.

We are drifters.
This lake, these rivers are county borders,
Of these times and tracks with trains on wires,
Within this quiet settlement,
I'm surrounded by everyone and everything I've ever known.

One hundred and fifty years.
A stumbling history
From a night shift without radio,
A town without community
To the inter-urban train whistle,
Conceding the shift from farms to factories.

My grandfather spoke of hardship,
Growing up mean and strong,
baling hay and shoveling coal
For two dollars a day.

My grandmother lifted her eyes from her victory garden
As her elders arrived by horse and buggy
Providing homemade dairy from Jackson Center
A promise kept every week.

In my time I've missed what used to be;
The picnics and playgrounds,
The smallness of childhood,
Before the invaders from the north.

Still, with familiarity and family,
Close proximity yet ample distance from the grand city,
The amazing sands of protected lands.
There must be something here.
Every time I've had the opportunity to leave,
I've chosen to stay.

Praise Be To Crows

Jessica Thompson (Posey County)

Let it be late autumn.
Let there be a small town.

Let it be surrounded by cornfields.
Let there be crows.

Let their numbers be incalculable.
Let neither laser nor cannon send them away.

Let them settle inside the eaves of our houses.
Let them sleep in the tops of our trees.

Let silos spill over with shiny black feathers.
Let the fields grow dark with wings.

Let it be done.
Let the machinery be silenced.

Praise be to crows.

Pulaski County

Mary Lee Gutwein (Pulaski County)

Home Again in Indiana, down 421 Highway
Cruising along singing that song
You'll see romance with a quick glance,
Of summer wheat waving as birds of a feather
Twirl through the blue of spring's
Fresh warm weather in County Pulaski.
The County Seat, Winamac, means "Catfish" from Indian days.
Now the Indians battle under Friday night lights.
Still a fisherman's tasty catch as the river
Flows south on its path past 200 years ago
Pioneer dreams that came true.
Spend a spell in our local Tippecanoe River State Park.

Monterey is a wonder town of 218 strong and happy folk.
Take delightful and back country roads, because,
One wonders where it is.
Wet your whistle at Root Beer Stand or Dairy Queen.
Like Pulaski, Star City, Denham, and more
The trip is worth it. These villages are a "must be seen"
Go West side 421 through Medaryville.
Called "Tater Town" growing with potential.
A new shiny store, welcomes you.
"The Small Town with a Big Heart"
Francesville sits too on 421.
That 1800's cattle trail became a major busy highway.
Seven churches, all promote God's Word, your soul to save.
1000 Residents, as in parade, to everyone they wave.
For years they celebrate Fall Festivals and Spirit Day
The Trojans guard their fields in the sporting way.

Mapping the Muse

Honest to goodness county country living is enjoyed
By 8 out of 10 of our current 13,408 folk
On a good day and that's no joke.
"Relax", the word that farmers blend
With dedication as they tend
To family and promise of the land.
Crops in straight lines grow fast.
It is the incredible gift
Of an autumn sun just before harvest
Shining on the Canyons of Corn in Pulaski County
To make you glad you came.

Fog

Joseph Heithaus (Putnam County)

1.

On corn stubble
a softness how
she rounds each barb
on the fence sings so
we can hardly hear
her honey music
barely see through
her smoke barely
open our own mouths
to mouth our own
sweetness you can
barely hear
us

2.

When she lifts its like
nothing's underneath her
the ground naked the juniper
with her blue
everything uncovered
the stone inside the stone
shivering white whispering
remove or *place here*

Too many holes enough
burial   we want some
of our children back
you want to lift
yourself out   disappear

How Ripley County Came To Be

Cathy May (Ripley County)

Long before Indians or white men
Lived a giant like race of men
They built mounds of earth
These men of wide girth
And were never heard from again.

Then Indian tribes were everywhere
Shawnee, Miami and Delaware
They lived off the land
The hunting was grand
The fishing, none could compare.

In 1673 came Robert La Salle
A Frenchman who followed a trail
Soon fur traders came
To this land with no name
And built forts that could withstand a gale.

Comes the Revolutionary War
One hundred eight troops came from afar.
They were captured here
Colonel Laughery did fear
He had lead his troops in too far.

Eleazer Ripley was famous.
An Army General was he, plus
His grandfather founded
Dartmouth College abounded
Ripley County was named on this basis.

John Depauw donated one hundred acres
Filled with Maples and Walnuts and Firs.
Creates a county seat
Whose beauty can't be beat.
Ripley County, your natives' hearts stir.

Ask Me Sometime - I'll Show You My Cow

Don A. Wright (Rush County)

As a child, I grew up, by the side of the road,
in a handsome new house, an expansive abode.

Farmers we were and still farmers yet –
all manner of animals, but not one my pet.

"They'd be snarling and noisy and under my feet,
I can hardly imagine the profit they'd eat"

so saith my father, I remember him now –
so I went to the barnyard and picked me a cow.

Now a cow is most useful and makes quite a pet.
This is my secret, I have no regret.

A cow will come running and gratefully too,
to unburden her milk and contentedly chew.

She has no contempt for the names you might give her,
change it ever so often and plan to out live her.

A cow can lay down but mostly will stand,
and do what it wants, but not on command.

And don't try to ride her, she's not saddle broke,
but tell your friends they can do it, it's good for a joke.

A cow for a pet? At least a good friend –
she shared all she owned, right up to the end.

For one day a cow and the butcher must meet,
just don't name a pet you're intending to eat.

I cherished her friendship and the kinship we felt,
so I made her stay with me as shoes and a belt.

A billfold and gloves and many shoelaces –
I've carried her with me to so many places.

She was my pet, just a memory now –
ask me sometime – I'll show you my cow.

Magnetic Healer

Thomas Alan Orr (Shelby County)

The black shay, pulled by onyx-colored horses,
Stopped in the dooryard and he stepped out,
A tall black-hatted figure in a long black coat.
The children ran and hid as he went to the door.

He was known in these parts, among the farms
And villages along Blue River, revered and reviled,
True healer or conniving quack, depending
On the daily run of gossip at the general store.

He treated humans, horses, the occasional cow –
Blood circulation, broken bones, hysteria,
The assorted aches and pains resulting,
So he said, from misalignment with cosmic forces.

They showed him where she lay, stomach distended,
Barely awake. He lifted her eyelids, took her pulse.
He swept the magnets across her belly, drawing off,
He said, the bad electric fluids that made her suffer.

Within the hour she awoke, her swelling down.
She took some broth. Her father pressed a silver dollar
Into the healer's palm. He tipped his hat and left,
Trailing a whiff of whiskey and stale tobacco.

Whenever the healer attended church, he sat
In the furthest pew, bundled in his long black coat,
Hat removed, sad eyes fixed on the wooden cross,
Fingering the magnets, poles reversed, pushing outward.

From Coral to Coal: the Making of Spencer County

Peggy Brooks (Spencer County)

Ancient Seas, layers of sediment
Eons of time create buried sunlight
Fuels of the future

Rivers form and carve channels
Flood and retreat make soils rich
Forests form.

Animals abound:
Panthers scream and bears roam
Bison seek salt licks while
Turkey & deer silently stalk

People come
Land is divided; sold by lots and
Recorded in land offices
Farmers bring families
Forests yield when crops are planted

Communities grow
Mills and stores; schools and churches
Named for founders or features:
Little Pigeon Creek, Springville, Grandview
Or Gentryville, Chrisney, Newtonville

Commerce develops as the nation grows
Politics polarize and neighbors debate
Young men argue, conflicts arise

War divides and soldiers die
Spencer County's favorite son assassinated
The nation heals as states spread
Industry beckons and mining delves

Mapping the Muse

Modern age brings stable population
Agriculture dominates but tourism leaps
Legendary faces, legendary places

Iconic place names of Lincoln City and Santa Claus
Recreation draws and summer brings crowds
Winter relapses, quiet returns.

Home beckons, and families are rich.
Children return and raise new families.
Sleepy villages with churches full.
Our Spencer County home.

The Farmer

Carol Rupley (St. Joseph County)

Just like that, the mercury lights turned the countryside silver grey
In predawn, the farms across St. Joe Valley glowed
like lanterns scattered across the landscape
Silent, but for muted cows
The barn stood against the sky in silhouette
A sky just turning yellow on the horizon line

Overslept, again, when there was work!
No matter the rush, always late, always 'overslept'

Grandpa had already crossed back from the barn
And in the back room, placed muddy boots carefully in their spot
Grandma hurried around the kitchen
Cooking eggs over-easy, frying bacon
The aroma filled the room
As did the sound of the radio
Set loud for her faulty hearing

"For the Midwest Farm Report, all indicators are up..."

A morning staple, daily ritual
He always listened

"And in a national rivalry that goes back decades,
Notre Dame beat Michigan 28 to 19..."
We both smiled

"Wake me tomorrow Grandpa, I want to help!" my voice melded with the radio din
But he never woke me...said I needed to sleep
For school

Just like that, we started another day, every day

I left for school...
And made him proud,
School, a scholarship, a degree earned

But after years, we are more than ever
Have more than ever
Except, I can't help but cross back to a kitchen flooded in warmth
Mercury lights at dawn and
The deep-rooted core of who we are

85

Starke County, USA

Carol Grubbs (Starke County)

Once surrounded by Indians,
In the marshy, wet land,
Starke County was founded,
And today, we yet stand.

In the heart of Kankakee Valley,
Where many folks live,
There are forests and rivers,
With so much to give.

The towns aren't real large,
But have much hope in their view;
We struggle at times,
But many smaller towns do.

There are festivals and parades,
Special times of the year;
Many people do gather,
Coming from far and from near.

We are a county of tradition,
And a county with heart;
We stand as a whole,
And most do their part.

We have Libraries and churches,
And Restaurants and bars;
At night, not so crowded,
That we can't see the stars.

Many years have passed,
Since John Starke did arrive;
Little did he know then,
That his dream would survive.

The Riches of Sullivan County

Nick Boone (Sullivan County)

What value's in the soil? Many drive past farmland
they've never worked, and think it boring. There's no action there.
No money. At Easter kids will play with baskets
full of plastic, manufactured eggs, and who will know,
as I do , the thrill of scaring a duck off its nest,
and who will have been scared half to death by the turkey
nearly stepped on in the woods near Minnehaha,
her brown-blue dappled eggs left there to inspect?
All this happens off-road, in farm country, Sullivan County,
one of the poorest in the state, they say.
But the riches it's given would take a lifetime to sing.

How many have been blessed to see a clan of mink
cross a gravel road? How much could be charged for that?
Or to have seen the black and silver sheen of a channel cat
in the flashlight's beam? Is there no value in night fishing?
Or in catching a score of small bass on nothing but the flash
of our naked hooks when we'd tired of threading hoppers?
Is there no value in a boy's discovering carp in Rainbow Lake,
like salmon, swim upstream to spawn, jumping up
the little waterfalls, smashing their fins against the rocks?
No value in the scores and scores of Northern Harriers,
Rough-Legged Hawks, and Short-Eared Owls that hover over marshes.
veering and swooping against the winds that skim across the pits?

Mapping the Muse

One Sunday morning I woke up early well before church,
to hike back to the big ravine that dropped off the edge
of our cornfield and where I'd spotted deertracks
and evidence of beaver by the stream at the bottom.
And here is something no one's ever seen,
no one but me one April morning, Sullivan County:
sipping from the stream below, a gigantic buck
raised his horns and shot up the side of the cliff
as if it were a football field. No one has these
jewel-lined memories, no one can reft me
of these riches, a string of pearls around my heart.

I've left my home, now twenty years, to pursue money,
my career. And once when I came back I went to Merom Bluff
and sat on the low stone wall and rang softly to myself
of these riches left behind, riches so few know
as the Wabash gleamed golden below.

Our Homeland

B.J. Green (Switzerland County)

They crossed the river with highest hopes
Waded the narrows and paddled their boats
Some came cross land with horses and ox
Others walked the forest and fields of the fox
The land they could see was hilly and level
Some land to farm the other to dwell in
They built their homes with logs from the trees
Rocks from the fields and bricks they had baked
Blacksmiths and millers, hunters and farmers
They needed them all to grow the land stronger
Some brought the vines to plant on the hills
And later made wine from the grapes they had tilled
Hay was the cash crop sent downriver to sell
Steamboats and flatboats carried it well
Our county grew and gave it their best
Mr. Meade designed a dam, that soon fed the West
We had a factory that made quality shoes
One built camper tops, others plastic molded for parts
Then a casino was built and a hotel grew there
The largest in Indiana or so we are told
Church spires and tree lined streets
Define Vevay our county seat.
If you just visit or come here to stay
You'll find you are welcome forever, or a day
Switzerland County a piece of our pride
I was born here, have lived here and in Switzerland clay I'll lie when I die.

Respect

Thomas O'Dore (Tippecanoe County)

six pallbearers riding
in a black Roadmaster Buick
silent \ as the mood upon us
my wife's grandmother
in the hearse ahead

winding out the city streets
toward a township cemetery
on the western Indiana prairie
near \ where the farm once stood
and the husband already lay

liquid August heat ripples
hot currents of apathy
above sidewalks and streets
few passing vehicles stop
one even breaks our ranks

but one pedestrian old man
at mid-block stops \ stands erect
and doffs his hat

Shrinking Acres

Ben Rose (Tipton County)

Break open this land and
find the deep heart of us.
We bare many things in silence
giving emotions a simple nod or wink at best.
But this land holds genetic
markers of memory a collective resonance,
immigrant vines of tomato sweat,
pigs cattle soy and wheat.

We Pioneer the hybrid seeds of change
back into tired Earth,
combing its dirty hair into neat rows,
spraying more chemicals
to hold organisms in place
like a worn out comb over.
We curse the corporations who
muscled our birthright away,
leaving us to assemble parts
in a machine we used to own.

The First Drive

Ruth Frasur (Union County)

The first drive from Indianapolis to Liberty. 465 to 74 to 44.

The endless fields.

The shriveling towns.

Not even towns.

Enclaves of houses, new and old, garages and sheds. The skeletons of barns. The mummified mills of a time gone by. A living soul here and there seeming like a remnant of some forgotten population left struggling against the relentless onslaught of time and decay.

So much sun. So much fog. So much wind. Not enough trees to slow any of it down or provide any protection.

Post Road.

Acton Road.

Don't take the first exit to Shelbyville. Take the next one...or is it the next one?

Manilla.

Manilla?

Homer.

Rushville. This is excruciating. I'm so glad that little store in Manilla had Little Debbies.

Glenwood. Will this drive NEVER end? I should have stopped for gas in Rushville.

Connersville. Oh, I've heard of this. But never mind. I just saw a sign.

Liberty. 12 miles. I should have checked the oil before I left. Please don't break down in Connersville. How would I explain that? Who would I explain it to? Can I walk to Liberty from Connersville. Should I just walk back to Indianapolis? I'm young. I could do it. It'd only take a day or two, right? On, never mind. The temperature gauge looks closer to normal now. I'll remember to buy oil in Liberty.

Liberty.

I'm going to Liberty. My Love is in Liberty. He's there, and I'll drive through this ridiculous, godforsaken land with bare earth and too much sun and too much wind and not enough trees and not enough water if it means I reach him.

But wait.

The road winds here.

The earth bucks up and down.

The forest that used to rule here fights back against the desolation. I can breathe better somehow.

Is it because he's here?

Yes.

No.

Yes and no. Yes or no.

It's this land. It's this place.

And here I am...at the top of what I thought was just another rise.

No. This is the top. This is the vantage point from which Liberty begins to greet me and from which I greet it.

Above the East Fork—not yet knowing the name.

Mapping the Muse

Cresting the hill and seeing the earth and water and the rebellious, living, fighting forest open up to welcome me. Leaving behind the parched and dusty road and falling into the arms of something that can only be home. A world separated from the apocalypse by a fork in the rive and a valley cut by ancient waters.

A forgotten county with little to recommend it to its more cultured and heritage siblings.

An overlooked patch of land preserved by its geography nurturing my Love and sparking my love.

Preparing my home and preparing me for home.
Whispering of a past not so distant and not so full of regret.

Promising rest and protection from the winds that haunt the fields and the highways.

Playing an ocean symphony through the leaves and singing a song of joy and hope.

The first drive of many. The first strand of a rope ever strengthening, tautening, luring, ensnaring, pulling me home.

[In 1993, Ruth Frasur met her husband at the University of Indianapolis. A native of Michigan, she was often disoriented by the alien terrain of Indiana, which seemed so flat and barren. When her then-boyfriend moved back to his hometown, she did what any lovesick, impulsive college student would do: she set out to see him in her 1983½ Mercury Lynx. She found more than a man on that first trip. Ruth has now lived in Union County for nearly 20 years and has nearly raised three sons with the man she was driving toward on that first drive.]

Giving a Reading in Indiana
Rob Griffith (Vanderburgh County)

How strange to wake in the middle of the night
in a bedroom small and tidy as a monk's cell,
to step outside and find yourself alone
beneath a bowl of stars, the sound of surf
a whisper in the fields. What currents, winds
have beached your ship in all this green, this sea
of corn? What trackless paths have brought you here?

In the morning, you'll rise and read some poems
to sleepy undergrads. Some will doze;
some will rub their eyes and think of lunch, or tests,
or the perfect slope of a girl's neck
in the second row; and some, a very few,
will slowly wake and find them lovely,
a burst of sunlight on a rocky shore.

Vermillion County Tableau

Gary Cowan (Vermillion County)

Indians flowing with a timeless river.
Pioneers weaving through an ageless forest.
An arduous trek, a beacon in the dark
for all those who dare to follow.

The poetry and steel symmetry of vehicles
from a storied, yet distant past,
storming the gently sloping hills of Newport
like a conquering army atop a crested butte.

Frightened immigrants in a foreign land,
leaving the familiar for a different dream.
Odious labor in the dankness of the mines
and uncertain futures as budding merchants ply their wares.

Yet what connects them also comforts them
The flow of their native tongue.
The tidy garden, redolent and florid.
The sauces replete with spice and exotic flavor, the vine that elates.

Then these proud people, laughing, lachrymose with nostalgia,
ever mindful of time honored traditions,
slowly embrace an Americana, this Vermillion County
that connects them to a new reality and a new wealth of dreams and hope.

With the clatter of Bocce ball amidst the laughter and lilt of Italian,
the crack of a bat, the thud of a ball in a mitt.
With the soaring voice of a joyous Italian tenor,
the shouts of children frolicking in a swimming pool.

A proud festival evokes the past.
Newly exotic aromas and tastes beckon, along with the warm, familiar recipes,
but timeless spirits still beckon to us and hauntingly call out in a whisper,
embracing us from across the windswept prairie.

But will we listen to that voice that touches us in silent, reflective times?
Or will today's daily bustle muffle and mute those gentle, yet insistent promptings?
Our past forever seeks to touch us, to connect us to the divine
With its subtle, eternal voice asking only to be heard.

Indiana Sestina

Mark Minster (Vigo County)

Our house hunches back of a little hill
of siltstone, alluvium, and glacial till
with a hardwood canopy that trades off stars
for nuts and barred owls: it's not much but it's ours:
a hidden notch, a hollow where our children
wade and swim in a jewelweed ocean

popping seedpods. We live far from the ocean
I fell in love with, Big Sur, steep scrub oak hills,
the scent of spray and sage. But we have children
here in the heartland, where it's your job to till
and harvest and my job to teach and ours
to show our kids the measureless world, from stars

between branches to napkins under forks. The stars
last night's neighborhood jog were an ocean
swelling after sunset. I stayed out for hours
under the ecliptic, on top of our hill,
to watch Arcturus and Spica flip on, till
I could see past all the floodlights. Our children

dreamed, she in her crib, he his bed, what children
dream. You sent texts. I caught my breath with stars,
running off the summer's anger, running till
I could conjure the cold Pacific Ocean
under Pico Blanco, each coastal hill
of ceanothus and toyon, dark hours

of night-walks and dawn-hikes all mine, all hours.
It's so much harder and better, having children,
being with you, than hiking chaparral hills
alone, no flashlight, ridge-edge, between stars
and the reckless equanimity of ocean.
Some love grows in serpentine, some roots in till,

some love's a vista, and some zeroes in till
it's a leeward hollow as sheltered as ours,
tucked in and away as far from open ocean
as you can imagine, tucked in like children.
Sometimes it seems there are only so many stars.
That's the floodlights' fault, the thick trees on our hill.

I keep running till I come home down the hill
to you, to our children, to our little ocean.
There are infinite stars, none of them, all of them ours.

Wabash County – A Community of Light
Nancy Bell (Wabash County)

How I wish you could have been here experiencing the awe of an excite crowd.
When, at the flick of a switch, the sky lit up making a multitude of people very proud.
Wabash, Indiana had become the first electrically lighted city,
One of many accomplishments for the county and its various entities.

Light is our mantle. Like a constant beam, our towns and cities glow
With beauty, prosperity, and goodwill, helping our communities grow.
The city of Wabash is the county seat where people with needs often gather.
The magnificent courthouse, perched stately on a hill, shines light in all kinds of weather.

The Light of Knowledge is available to people of all ages and yearnings.
Ivy Tech College and Manchester University provide excellent academic learning.
Our five libraries are a hub of activity and information,
And places of faith provide spiritual truths for contemplation.

The Light of History is found in historical museums with technology of cutting edges,
The Treaty of Paradise Spring Historical Park, Stockdale Mill, and covered bridges,
The Ford Home with a medical museum, and the Wabash Erie Canal Lock,
Vice President Thomas Marshall's home, and Hanging Rock.

The Light of Culture graces the county with arts of amazing grandeur.
Nationally acclaimed entertainers perform in Cordier Hall and the Ford Theatre.
Entertainment is superb at the Honeywell Center, the Honeywell House,
the restored Eagles Theatre, and an old-time Drive-In Movie. Jamming at Modoc's Market,
The Noisemaker, or the Firehouse is ideal for the young and groovy.

The Light of Fitness and Fun is high on the list with two reservoirs and beautiful lakes,
Bicycle trails, river walks, numerous sports, and a top-notch YMCA,
Public parks, swimming pools, town festivals, and the county 4-H Fair,
Promote family, good health and well being for people everywhere.

The Light of Economics comes through business, farming, and industry
Which provide an income for daily living and a county of prosperity.
The Light of Service is perhaps the most valued asset to date.
People helping people is what makes Wabash County great.

We hope you'll come and visit awhile, and perhaps stay to live.
Hop on a bike, a bus, or a car and see what our county has to give.
And let's not forget, come 2016, to light a candle for the state of which we are a part
And celebrate the birth date of Indiana, the homeland dear to our heart.

Visiting The Past

Marcy Meyer Johnson (Warren County)

I love to sit and listen to the old folks reminisce
As they recall the old days, their memories are of this ...
They fuss about who lived where and funny things they did —
They walk me down the streets again, where memories can't stay hid ...
It's all right there in front of me — Stellie Powell outside his store —
Then up to Elsie's Dry Goods, bells jingle at the door ...
She steps out from the back and I buy some sour balls —
Say "Goodbye!" and head on out, there is much to be recalled ...
What a beautiful day it is, Maralee waves from the bank —
I stop down at the station and put a dollar in my tank ...
I take in all the scenery, homes and cars of yesterday —
Fresh air and memories push me on, as I make my way ...
The old schoolhouse is quiet, class must be in session —
I step up and take a peek inside as the kids take in their lesson ...
Ol' Annie's cookin' something good, the flavor fills the air —
I take a seat upon a swing, look up at it and stare ...
That school has seen it all, no doubt, helping old and young alike —
It gave them what they needed, to get going good in life ...
The Sweet Shop's open, Earl Berkshire slices pie,
And he makes sure I try a piece before I say goodbye ...
My trip is almost over, a haze clouds up my view —
I park the car aside the curb and step back into the "new."
BUT WAIT !!!
I am being pulled back there again, and I eagerly go with it —
What is this? You're kidding me!
Ol' Joe gave me a ticket ?!!?

Read For Our Bicentennial

Betty A. Stanley (Washington County)

Read about the journey,
And those travelers who came,
To settle this freedom land,
A region yet to choose a name,

Read about the pioneers' courage,
They had to be hardy and brave,
The wilderness was unknown,
Of themselves they gave.

Read about the lives they lived,
Each one worked and made their way,
They struggled and labored to make a home,
Liberty allowed them their say.

Read about the hardships,
The toil and suffering they shared,
With others who, like themselves,
Had a vision, but they dared.

Read about the land they cleared,
And planted in the abundant earth,
They hunted the game and fished the streams,
Their dreams were giving birth.

Read about those who lived,
And those who died as well,
Their accomplishments were many,
Their stories too many to tell.

Read about the rejoicing,
The love as they could see,
Their dreams and hopes fulfilled,
Our land, for you and me,

Read about the passing years,
Our Bicentennial is now,
Salem and Washington County
We celebrate you, take a bow.

Bear in the Woods

Patricia D. Drischel (Wayne County)

A story told to me by my great-granny
Intrigued me so I took a trip to see her
Beloved Indiany
There in a dark, damp forest, a rusty
Iron fence enclosed three lichen covered
Stones that marked some of my
Ancestor's bones
The story had gone down from one to
Another 'bout how a bear came upon a
Father and sons...laboring hard at
Chores. And the women folk looking
Out of doors saw a ghastly sight
And they were helpless for the only gun
Leaned against a tree in the thicket.
Soon it would be night.
They prayed and cried, weak with
Sorrow and fright.
On the morrow, a man going through the
Country planting apple seeds came upon
The tragic scene.
He helped the women dig the graves and
Bury their dead.
Then looking toward the heavens, in a
Prayerful voice he said, Dear God,
We commit to Thy keeping these brave
Ones who have cleared the land and
Worked so hard and now they accept
Their reward. — Amen.
He planted apple seeds 'round the
Graves and to this day the apple
Trees are there by those dear ones
Killed by a bear.
And on a warm day, the apple blossoms
Gay fall on the ground and make a
Blanket on the sod like a caress from
The hand of the God.

Ouabache State Park (16 March 2003)

Doug Sundling (Wells County)

The clamor of geese
resonates with a spring melody.
The air dances
with the demise of winter.
The slushy, icy blanket
that entombs the lake
cannot run away
and waits helplessly
for the Spring sunshine
of this March day.

Off Keiser Road
Amy McVay Abbott (Whitley County)

Shy of the surface, yellow and blue wildflowers rest
Soon coaxed upward by the diffuse April sun.

Washington township farmers overturn the dark, bountiful Indiana soil
And renew the cycle of planting and harvest
As my ancestors long ago worked their field of dreams.

My arms filled with red roses, I visit old friends.
I share the first bud with Suzi who danced at my wedding
Her hair as red as the roses and her laughter filling the room.

I am surprised to find Pastor here.
He married us three decades ago at the country church over the hill.
Spires from St. John's and Eberhard churches rise over country fields
With bells signaling new life for nearly two centuries.

Our dear neighbors Kirby and Neva are here, reminding me of Kirby's wood shop,
Endless entertainment for nosy children from next door.

If it takes a village to raise a child, my village is here off Keiser Road.

Bea and Phil, and Doris and Kenny, and Scotty, Chris, Willis,
and dear, beautiful Julia, gone too soon,
together now in the springtime of this peaceful place
rooted in the rich earth and promise of Whitley County.

Their voices echo in my mind, recollections ebbing and flowing with the seasons.
Whispers in my memory, laughter and tears, ice cream socials and women's club,
Vacation Bible School and confirmation class, beginnings and endings.

Truly only memories endure here.
The stone is rolled away; what remains is temporal and fleeting.

In the autumn, the fields beside this place lay fallow,
Awaiting the hope and resurrection the abundant earth promises.